GAUDÍ

editorial **escudo de oro, s.a.** Palaudarias, 26 - 08004 Barcelona - Spain

PROLOGUE

This book, in the beauty of its illustrations and in the profundity of its succinct text, offers us a remarkable explication of the significance of the master architect Antonio Gaudí and his works.

Here we see and are told how Gaudí in each new project "returned to the origin" as he would say and worked out a new solution — different from all of his previous constructions — in order to meet the special circumstances of the task facing him at that point. And as time passed he came closer and closer to what we can see was his inevitable destiny: to unite as never before in the history of arcchitecture the *form* and the *structure* of the environmental objects that he was erecting so that they would in turn — in form, color, and texture — approximate nature itself. And specially that nature of which Catalonia is composed: scaring peaks, sturdy trees, rocky shorelines, sunny strands, and rolling waves of iridescent water.

The breakthrough in Gaudí's development out of the historicism that had plagued nineteenth-century architecture came soon after 1900 while he was designing the Casa Calvet chairs and benches, the Park Güell gatehouses, and was beginning to project the church proposed for the Colonia Güell at Santa Coloma de Cervelló. In his renovation of the Casa Batlló, in his construction of the Casa Milá, and then in his study for the Passion façade of the Sagrada Familia church, we can see that he succeeded in achieving a truly "equilibrated" structure, just as in the same years he attained a calm equilibrium in his own life by dedicating it wholly to the designing of one of the greatest churches in Christendom.

Salvador Tarragó is one of the most penetrating of the new young minds that have applied themselves to analyzing and evaluating the works of Gaudí. Having grown up in the era of renewed enthusiasm for his architecture, they are concerned ultimately with determining the meaning that this Catalan genius of the recent past may hold for the creative present. Tarragó's analysis of Gaudí's œuvre is made in terms of the psychology of the architect, the special problems or programme involved in each project, and the significance of the resultant structure as *architecture*. For its attention to these particular aspects, the present book is outstanding among the many publications that have appeared in recent years about the Catalan master. For instance, the author's socio-political examination of the forces that generated the Church of the Sagrada Familia is a unique contribution and will do much to explain the nature of Catalanism to those visitors to Barcelona who are fortunate enough to read this volume.

One of the principal discoveries made by those who, after extensive study of the art of Gaudí, have come to the realization that he was not only a person dedicated obsessively to his profession and to whom his architecture was Life and his life was Architecture, but also that he was fundamentally a rationalist in the way in which he operated. The exuberance of his works actually obtains from his conviction, as Tarragó points out, that there is a rational order of a higher geometry which both underlies nature and signified the sacred; it was not fantasy, nor egoistical expression, nor surrealism that generated Gaudí's forms, but rather a dogged search for quintessential reality.

George R. Collins
Columbia University
New York
President "Amigos de Gaudí" · USA

(Photo: Brangulí.)

ORIGINS

The art and architecture of Gaudí are so personal and autobiographical that it is almost impossible to separate the work from its author as both offer mutually revealing aspects.

Born in Reus on 25th. June 1852 into a humble family, his father, grandfather and great grandfather were potters; these two factors were to determine Gaudí's life story.

His place of birth influenced his personality, defined by the converging of two antagonistic tendencies: a passionate nervous temperament, ("People of the countryside, people of lightning!") goes the popular aphorism, which also says: "...and the people of Reus - a handful of Jupiter's darts") combined with an ordered intelligence governing his energy, all of this is symbolically represented in the horned head of Jupiter Ammon dominating the façade of the temple of Augustus, built where today stands the Cathedral of Tarragona.

The importance of his birthplace is also born out by the fact that almost all his colleagues in the architectural school which constituted his workshop for the Sagrada Familia were originally from the countryside around Tarragona.

Gaudí always considered his family tradition of potters as something basic, using it on many occasions as his main source for visualizing bodies in space and solving his problems in a direct way without needing any graphic aids or plans. This view, rather that of a potter, applied not to a plastic mass like crude clay, but to an elastic one such as copper, was to be the basis for the creation of this new architectural topology as shown in the roofing of the pavillions at the entrance to the Güell Park, the façade and terrace of the Casa Mila, the staircase courtyard of the Casa Batlló or the basements of the Güell Palace.

Medallion of Jupiter Ammon.
(Source: Tarragona
Archaeological Museum).

THE CIUDADELA PARK
(1876-1882)

After finishing his studies in 1878, and until he began the Casa Vicens, Gaudí devoted himself to work of a public nature with social implications; this, we wished to put into a special group so as to differentiate it from other phases in his life when he was engaged in work for private clients. It is a liberal and co-operativist Gaudí who takes part in the latest public works instigated by the Republic, before immersing himself almost completely in the long period of the Restoration of the Monarchy.

He began to work even before finishing his studies, first as a talented draughtsman, and later as an assistant in the firm of the master Josep Fontseré i Mestres. He also worked in some architectural businesses such as that of F. Villar, the author of the first project for the Sagrada Familia, so as to be able to pay for his studies.

On the land belonging to the grim military fortress which General Prim —also from Gaudí's region— had handed over to the city of Barcelona, the Ciudadela Park was built, representing a hymn of joy and liberty after the oppression that had been undergone. Fontseré, who had won a competition organized by the Municipality and who did some fine work in the newly urbanized areas like the market "El Born" and the "Umbráculo", obtained Gaudí's collaboration in several undertakings in the Park.

Although Gaudí's direct participation has only been able to be proved in the building of the monumental fountain, the balustrade in the small square dedicated to Aribau, the water tank and the door and metal railings at the entrance to the park, it can be supposed that he also intervened in other aspects and details inside the Park.

Aerial view of the lake and fountain in the Ciudadela Park.

Fountain in the Ciudadela Park.

THE STREET LAMPS IN THE PLAZA REAL (1878-1879)

This fine porticoed square was built on land formerly belonging to the Capuchin convent, which was occupied during the Napoleonic invasion and handed over by Las Cortes in 1822 to the constitutionalist municipality.

This land remained undeveloped until 1848 when the architect Francesc Daniel i Molina took charge of the building of the square, coinciding with work on the opening of Ferdinand VII street. However, the gardens were not laid out until Gaudí had finished two projects in 1878 and specially designed the lamps for the square.

Thanks to his experience in wrought iron work gained

Aerial view of the Plaza Real.

in the work on the Ciudadela Park, Gaudí was able to undertake the construction of the lamps assured of his control and ability with the material, a surprising thing in so young an architect.

Furthermore, thanks to the memory of the candelabra project —published by C. Martinell in the book mentioned at the end— it can be appreciated how carefully and ingeniously he conceived these city lights:

''the shapes of the post (the axis of the lamp) are those a column must have, the lower end of this is put into the ground and the details of same should facilitate industrial operations necessary for the polishing and finish of the iron to avoid long work on smelting and moulding''.

This was always his way of working, constructive rationalism tempered by a great sensitivity.

Street lamp in the Plaza Real.

Plan of a kiosk cum public convenience for E. Girossi. (Source: I.M.H.B.)

THE LAMPS ON THE SEA WALL
(1880)

The diverse projects and city development plans carried out during this first period, if analyzed as a whole, and if all the rebuilding of the city carried out in those years is taken into account, we can see they are part of a movement whose goal was to transform the feudal walled city which Barcelona still was, into a modern capital.

After the impetus given to city development in Barcelona by pulling down of the city walls in 1854, the Cerdá plan for the Ensanche was a programme of urban development which, in spite of the sins of destruction it committed, served to direct the growth of the city for more than 100 years.

In the old part of the city, it was not until the "ominous citadel" was pulled down in 1869 that the process of urban transformation of the East side and the sea front was begun in 1878.

Gaudí played a direct part in these processes and also in the development of the most important public spaces, whether the planting of gardens in the Plaza Real (which really was no more than an excuse to manufacture a type of lamp appropriate for the illumination of the best streets and walks in Barcelona), or the installation of kiosks cum public conveniences which had been foreseen to be situated in twenty different places in the city.

In contrast, Gaudí, in 1905, once again began to interest himself in urban development on this same scale on the occasion of the development of the surroundings of the church of the Sagrada Familia incorporating it into the Jaussely Plan for Barcelona; but it was in mid Bourbon Restoration and at that time Gaudí's objectives were of a religious and monumental type, quite different from the secular and civic motivations he experienced in 1880.

Projected lights for the sea wall. (Source: Ràfols.)

To form an overall view of Gaudí's varied city projects in this first period, in spite of their being so isolated and dispersed, we must consider the plan drawn by Gaudí of the old town of Barcelona viewed from the sea, in which his idea of the city is synthesized.

The drawing shows an enormous esplanade reaching down to the sea, in place of the former sea wall, with eight tall lamps placed all the way along the front. These lamps, set out along the new sea front to serve as integral parts of the city-scape viewed from the land or from out at sea.

Barcelona, with this great garden platform open right down to the sea, giving a foretaste of what, eight years later, would be the Avenue of Palm Trees in the Universal Exhibition of 1888, would, with these large beacons some twenty metres in height, have given the striking impression of a superb modern industrial city.

Unfortunately, the greater part of these public ventures of Gaudí's did not come into effect. Due to his trips to Mataró in connection with work on the Mataró cooperative, Gaudí got to know the inventor Enrique Girossi, with whom, in 1878, he designed a complex city building destined to serve different purposes.

The front part could be a flower stall or a kiosk for the sale of drinks or newspapers, depending on its position in the city (although it was basically intended to be built in the Ramblas), while the rear part was always a public convenience.

On the sides were marble plaques and flat windows which contained varying types of information and served as an illuminated notice-board; the building had an enormous clock, a thermometer and a barometer.

The idea was to construct the building using cast iron pillars topped with an enormous protecting roof also of cast iron and glass, the roof panels being of marble and glass. At night the whole thing could be completely closed simply by lifting up the metalic blinds.

Position of the street lamps in the new urbanization proposed by Gaudí. (Source: Friends of Gaudí.)

THE MATARO COOPERATIVE
(1878-1882)

Mataró has a special significance both professionally and emotionally with regard to Gaudí's career. It has been mentioned that here, he made the acquaintance of Girossi, it is possible too that he established some contact with Manuel Vicens in this city, and finally, it is in the capital of the Maresme where he carried out his first project of real importance: The workers' quarter and the factory for the cooperative society "La Obrera Mataronense".

It was in this town too that he experienced the only love affair we know of, apart from the one related by

Joan Maragall as an allegory. According to one version, the affair did not come to anything because the girl was a Protestant, and, according to another, because the young lady finally decided on another man.

We will take this opportunity to state that a really human and sentimental study of Gaudí is yet to be made. The reasoned explanations given in general terms by Enric Casanelles appear, up to now, to be the most convincing, but Gaudí, that confirmed bachelor who lived with his father, until the latter died at the age of 90, and an orphaned niece (who died 6 years after the grandfather, of tuberculosis and being an alcoholic addicted to a patent medicine), we insist, still awaits a psychoanalytical study of a serious and objective nature.

We would guess that the conclusions to be reached from such a study could throw a very different light on his personality from the interpretations usually offered.

His complex and contradictory character is inseparable from his architecture, and in order to understand the latter one must be objectively aware of his personality and vice versa; his architecture and art can reveal many facets of his personality.

Whatever the case, his extraordinary humanity, his great capacity for loyalty and his moral and patriotic integrity are beyond all doubt, as is his stature in his profession and as an artist.

Gaudí's ideology during this first phase of urban activity, was determined by his collaboration with the directors of the Mataró co-operative.

Both the intensely Republican years in Reus, and his University period inclined him to identify with their principles. But, as asually happened with worker directors at that time, their co-operativism and community spirit had not yet developed into scientific socialism; they were on the side of ideological solidarity with diluted christianity, as their slogans written on the walls of the meeting hall in the co-operative proclaimed: "There is nothing greater than brotherhood", "Friend! Be loyal, practise kindness", etc.

Fragment of the façade of the casino in the "Obrera Mataronense" project. (Source: E. Casanelles.)

THE CASA VICENS
(1878-1885)

Two very important events proceeded from the construction of this summer holiday house for Manuel Vicens, the tile merchant: one which brought serious repercussions on a personal level, and another of great importance for the history of architecture. Gaudí had received his first important commission from a private client; this represented a significant turning point in his professional life (as he came in contact straight away with Count Güell) as well as in his own mental development, if we bear in mind that when beginning work on the Casa Vicens, he was also starting on the Sagrada Familia with its consequent religious influence. Also, with the construction of this house, Modernism (also termed *Art Nouveau, Jugendstil, Secession,* etc.) was born, and the list of a long series of projects and buildings in which Gaudí, deriving his inspiration mainly from Arab and Arab-Christian architecture, tried for the first time to find an outlet for architectural eclecticism.

Built between 1883 and 1885, although the plans were made in 1879, the house was enlarged and restored —especially the garden— in 1925 by the architect Serra Martínez. Its greatest charm, among the many it possessed was, without doubt, the gallery overlooking the garden, now completely transformed.

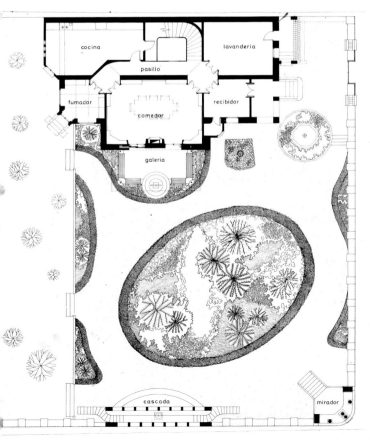

View of the garden in the Casa Vicens before restoration. (Source: Bergós.)

Ground floor of the Casa Vicens as built by Gaudí. (Source: A.H.U.A.D.)

Overall view of the Casa Vicens with the additions carried out in 1925.

Detail of the façade at attic level with ventilation holes.

Detail of the ceramic covering on the rows of brick binding the masonry wall.

Detail of the railing on the gate.

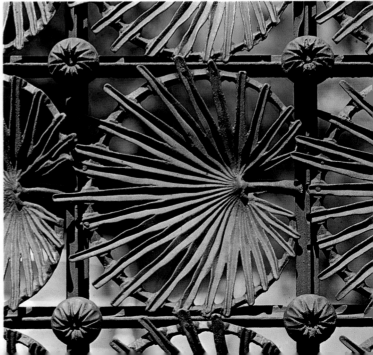

Entrance.

Detail of
the ceiling
on the
garden
gallery.

Ceiling of small smokers' lounge.

Fragment of the ceiling of the dining room with motifs in cardboard inspired by the fruits of the cherry tree.

Door leading into the garden from the smokers' lounge.

Details of the dining room.

Entrance to the house built for Máximo Díaz de Quijano, popularly known as "The Caprice", in Comillas (Santander).

THE GÜELL PAVILIONS
(1884-1887)

With the prolongation of the Diagonal towards the end of the twenties, the Güell estate was divided into two parts; and was on the site of what is now the University City. The Royal Palace of Pedralbes is the former country house of the Güells, but restored. Gaudí built the pavilions at the entrance to the estate, with the porter's lodge on the left and the stables on the right, also the railings and another two gateways together with some interior modifications, and restauration of the terrace of the old house. In 1887, when these buildings were under construction, the Diagonal terminated in the Plaza de Calvo Sotelo, which was why Count Güell ordered what is now the Paseo de Manuel Girona to be opened up, in order to gain entrance to his estate; the Paseo de Manuel Girona began in the Carretera de Sarriá and ended just in front the gate of the "Drac" (dragon).

Gateway and stables of the Güell Pavilions.

Basing his inspiration on the long mediterranean tradition of mud houses, Gaudí succeeded in improving the old method in a constructive way. For this, he used brick in those parts of the building which had structural functions (corners, apertures, cornices, etc.) and filled the hollow parts left in the brick construction with mud. The rain water, as in some examples of popular Moroccan architecture, runs off the corners by means of pipes which overhang. The simplicity of the old stables with their clear style of architecture defined by the broad parabolic arches, contrasts with the profusely decorated exteriors. But it is precisely this contrast which allows us to begin to interpret the problematic nature of Gaudí's architecture. By analysing his works, it can be observed that, from the outset, his architectural research developed in two directions which he considered to be inseparable: the search for structure together with an attractive surrounding plasticity. Thus, during this first stage, while Arab art interested him in its essentially decorative aspect, Gotich art attracted him for its stone structures.

View of the restored area of the stables, the horses' feeding troughs can still be seen.

Either because he couldn't develop both aspects, the structural and the plastic, to an equal level of excellence acceptable to him, or on account of the different difficulties that stood in the way of attaining complete success in both, or for some other reason, his search for structure and form certainly did develop at an uneven rhythm.

At times, as in the Astorga Palace, structural considerations prevailed, while in the Casa Calvet, the basic concerns were those of composition and form; it was only after long experience dating from the Casa Vicens to the Casa Calvet that he succeeded in uniting these two aspects of his work in one integral construction, as occured in his later works.

For this reason, the Güell Park, the Casa Batlló, the Casa Milá and the Crypt of the Güell colony are the best examples of what has been termed the Gaudiesque style.

We can verify all this in the case of the Güell pavilions, where he still used the Arab-christian inspired façade, while the interior could be described as early Gaudí.

Overall impression of the stable pavilion.

Inside the rotunda of the stables pavilion.

◁ *Entrance to the Güell Pavilions.*

Güell Pavilions: fragment of the entrance.

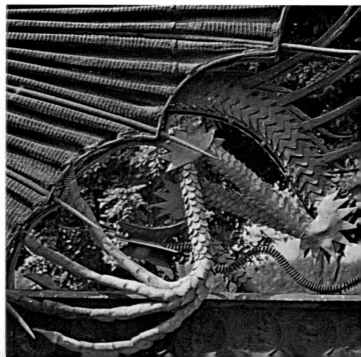

The young Gaudí is obsessed by the dragon theme. From his earliest works as a colleague of Fontseré's on the Ciudadela Park fountain and in the series illustrated here, he never ceased to introduce it as a decorative element. This aspect of his composition reached its pinnacle of expression in that work of art of the bloomery fire, which is the gate to the Güell pavilions.

The monster here assumes such importance that it looks as if the gate had been made for the express purpose of holding a dragon of these dimensions and not the reverse, that is, the dragon being a decorative element on a gate primarily intended as an entrance and exit.

The connection of this dragon with Saint George and the maiden should also be pointed out, as the lower part of the gate has a checkerboard of roses. After ridding himself of this fixation, the dragon theme is still to be found in some of his works, but it is either a completely domesticated animal and almost appealing, as in the case of the dragon on the staircase in the Güell Park, or it has been transformed into a mere allusion, as in the large dragon's backbone on the roof of the Casa Batlló. Gaudí must have acquired this theme which survived in popular culture as a remnant of an ancient animist cult, according to which, animals are the incarnation of transcendental spirits (suffice it to consider the old symbolist tradition of the dove, lamb, owl, serpent, and lion, etc...)

This theme, pagan in origin, was conveniently christianized by Gaudí, and as in the Sagrada Familia, the theme appears successively until it acquires a more refined expression as a symbolic dragon-demon caught placing a bomb in the hand of an anarchist worker as observed in the sculpted group depicted on one of the projections on the archways of the Rosary Chapel.

Ventilators and small dome on the Güell Pavilions.

THE TERESIAN COLLEGE (1888-1890)

As the same time as he was engaged in building the sumptuous Güell Palace, Gaudí conceived, between 1888 and 1890, this austere teaching college, which is a magnificent example of rationalism in construction. The quality of the materials used and the simplicity of line of the building become perfectly integrated in the construction, following rational lines. In this building, as in the later façade of the Güell Palace, the divergence that existed in the Güell pavilions does not become apparent.

As the budget was limited and the religious order austere in character, there was no attempt at decorating the façade, thus the rational quality of the inside was projected onto the outside, making it one of Gaudí's most coherent works. For the reception of visitors, Gaudí constructed a small building to serve rather as a porch on the ground floor and as an observation room on the upper floors. This porch, now magnificently adorned with a climbing plant, has a wrought iron railing which constitutes, along with those at the entrance to the Güell pavilions and Güell Palace, the three key pieces in iron corresponding to Gaudí's first phase.

Overall view of the Teresian College.

Front wrought iron entrance to college. ▷

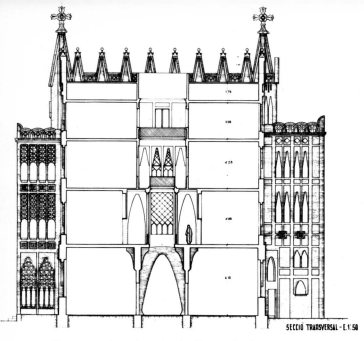

As a spatial expression of that rationalism in construction, there is nothing better than these long corridors. With the deep perspective formed by the indefinite repetition of the parabolic archways, the corridors form a perfect natural background for the walking to and fro of these hooded nuns, with whom they blend in perfect harmony. The first floor corridors along with the attic, the Bellesguard staircase and the part of the main floor extant in the Casa Batlló, with its private staircase, are some of the finest and most beautiful of Gaudí's creations.

Cross section done by L. Bonet Garí.

Detail of the parabolic archways in the corridor.

View of one of the side corridors on the first floor.

Overall view of the Güell Palace seen from the Nou de la Rambla street. The terrace in the foreground once belonged to the palace.

THE GÜELL PALACE
(1886-1891)

The contrast of such a luxurious building in such a crowded street as the Conde del Asalto —popularly known by the name of Calle Nueva de la Rambla— is due to the fact that the Güell family had for some time possessed a house in the Ramblas and two more where today the palace is situated, the passage linking the two buildings still being extant. The mansion refered to, besides being the family's city residence, was also a sort of museum for exhibiting their antiques, and a suitable background for the intense social life and activities which Eusebio Güell organized there.

Entrance with the Counts's coat of arms serving as a grille to the window in the porter's lodge.

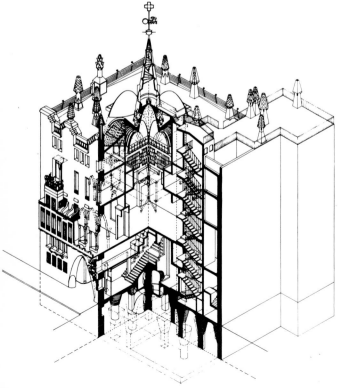

The basements of the Güell Palace were used as stables.

For this building, Gaudí studied more than twenty five plans for the façade from which he submitted two to be chosen by the owner who selected the one Gaudí himself preferred and which he later used.

The whole palace is supported at basement level by columns, with the exception of a few walls, so as to obtain maximum ventilation for the stables located on that floor.

There are more than forty different types of column in the entire mansion, from the heavy massive brick pillars in the basement, to the most varied collection of fine columns (made from Garraf marble), the majority of which were inspired by those in the Alhambra Palace, and can been seen in various key parts of the building.

The same inventive enthusiasm shows itself in the wide variety of roofs, windows, doors and other

Axonometric projection of the Güell Palace.   Dining room. ▷

architectural elements (the hanging stair case, the complex jut-window smoke-room, the chapel-cum-cupboard, the systems of ventilation and drainage, the organ, the room furniture etc.). All this is the product of a powerful architectural conception, its highest expression being the central courtyard which, with its double ceiling and starred dome, forms different levels and is an example, more than thirty years in advance, of Le Corbusier's free space concept.

Fragment of the coffered ceiling in one of the spare rooms overlooking the main façade.

Vault in the hall, with the windows on the floor where the bedrooms are located in the lower part.

Overall view of the terrace of the Güell Palace from the Nou de la Rambla street. The central cone covers the parabolic dome of the vestibule.

In the centre of the terrace there emerge the clear shapes of the archways in gradation, the parabolic dome and the conical dome superimposed, defining the complex system of balanced structures covering the central courtyard.

This space sets the tone for the whole of the interior of the building, because as the palace is situated in a narrow street and has no views of any interest on the opposite façade. Gaudí decided to direct the building onto the inside towards the aforementioned courtyard.

The enormous number of chimneys for ventilation, smoke extraction etc. is a unique sight on the rooftops of the old part of Barcelona. Gaudí, in a prelude to the urban spectacle afforded by the roofs of the Casa Batlló and the Casa Milá tried out a complex choral movement of abstract sculptures richly covered with glazed ceramic, marble or crystal, which were to surprise Picasso so much during his comings and goings to his studio in the same "carrer nou de la Rambla". Working on a commission of this nature, and only endeavouring to rationalize his function by introducing all possible improvements without so much as questioning the sense of constructing a palace 2,000 square metres in area, Gaudí showed that, from an ideological point of view, he was now integrated with the more conservative social strata, either religious or secular, for whom he worked exclusively.

Gradually, he came to acquire a more religious turn of mind, tending to look for the solution to his serious contradictions and those of the times in the mystic or stoic approach.

Thus, without questioning the established social system which as a young man he had often criticized, or ways of life, or the organization of city space, or any of those subjects so essential to the re-making of a modern city and twentieth century urban development, Gaudí concentrated all his energies on the attainment of a strictly stylistic goal, with the double demands of structural and plastic considerations already mentioned.

Indeed, in the Güell Palace we can appreciate how great his energy was (it explains how all this time was taken up with work and that he cared little about anything that was not his art) to have been able to create a style of architecture that was all his own and how difficult this was even for a personality such as his. While structurally he had now created a complete formal vocabulary of his own by means of the arches and parabolic domes; as regards the plastic element, when this structural theme did not determine form, he still borrowed many decorative elements and composite parts from, for example, arab art, as can be seen in some gates, wainscoting and balustrades.

Part of the towers and apse of the Sagrada Familia. ▷

One of the ventilators on the terrace.

Nativity façade.

The Sagrada Familia with the new Passion façade concealing part of the apse, work by Gaudí.

Detail of the sculpture, the Massacre of the Innocents.

THE SAGRADA FAMILIA
(1884-1926)

The parts of the Temple of the Holy Family built by Gaudí include the Crypt, the apse and the Nativity façade.

The construction of the new Passion façade was initiated by Gaudí's colleagues in 1952.

The best of the work done by Gaudí is mainly the Nativity façade, and such is the impact of this façade that it should be valued on its own, that is, as a building in itself.

Its architecture is reduced to pure symbolism so for this reason the criteria for the composition of this monumental modern altarpiece were for the most part sculptural.

Although the four towers are of fundamental importance, especially in an urban sense, the lower part of the façade with its allegorical aspects of the Nativity and the main stages in the life of Jesus shows a real religious dominance. In setting up this colossal nativity scene, the pedagogic will to christianize the masses is at its most effective and both Gaudi himself and the church works committee were conscious of this. Thus, the church, once it was finished —with its schools for the children in the neighbourhood, its workshops for the teaching of trades workmen, its catechistic work together with its liturgical functions— was destined to become an inspiring bastion of the Catholic faith; just at a time when the general process of dechristianization was a phenomenon produced by the industrial revolution and the ensuing social changes.

For this reason the Spiritual Association of the Devotees of Saint Joseph, the owners of the church, enjoyed from the outset the patronage and inspiration of Pope Leon XIII, who, by means of indulgences, blessings and even annual donations of half the money the Association collected all over the world and paid to the Vatican, gave impetus to the Building of this expiatory temple.

Detail of the Nativity façade with herald angels.

Gaudí took charge of the work when it had been started in accordance with the plans of the diocesan architect F. Villar.

This is why he had to accept the positioning of the church in the middle of the block with its axis parallel to the Calle Marina, while if he himself had begun the construction, it would have been positioned diagonally, along the axis of the avenue bearing Gaudí's name.

In this way, another large monumental urban unit would have been created with the San Pablo Hospital at the far end of the aforementioned avenue.

This desire to break with the quadrilateral style of Cerdá's Ensanche was set out in the Jaussely Plan drawn up in 1905 in which Gaudí collaborated by organizing the Temple surroundings.

The desire to open up diagonal streets as opposed to Cerdá's straight lines showed the modernistic tendency to make each part of the city different, to create dominant view points along axes of monumental symmetry so as to break the monotony of those infinitely parallel streets.

In this sense, the towers of the Sagrada Familia, reaching up amid all Cerdá's squareness, a hundred metres in height, and with the project for a central dome of a hundred and fifty metres, would have polarized and given shape to the city, symbolically christianizing the Barcelona landscape.

Today, with the chaotic situation of odd buildings crowding the city, and with the towers of the Besós Thermal station, 200 metres in height, the overall effect of the Sagrada Familia towers on the city skyline has been irredeemably lost.

The Sagrada Familia is the most popular and

Herald angels.

Night illumination, work of the engineer Carlos Bohigas.

internationally best known of Gaudí's works, and this obliges us to give it special consideration in this book. The silhouette of the four towers on the Nativity façade have become a symbolic sketch identifying Barcelona throughout the world, to such an extent that of the millions of tourist visiting the city annually, at least a third come to view this unfinished cathedral, even if they don't get out of the bus to do so.

The twenty films made about Gaudí and his work, some of which have been shown on european television, the 60 books with editions of nearly half a million copies, the approximately 2,000 newspaper articles published throughout the world with a minimum edition of 25 million copies, the million visitors to the 60 exhibitions held since 1910, the hundreds of thousands of foreign visitors who come to see his works, along with the thousands of studious *cognoscenti* who come to Barcelona specially, all these serve to demonstrate the phenomenon of Gaudí and his architecture on an ever-increasing mass scale.

Detail of the entrance of the Nativity façade.

This man, who despised publicity, who shunned all contacts that could imply personal advancement, who stayed in Catalonia voluntarily, has acquired a world-wide popularity equal to that of the foremost artists of our time: Picasso, Cézanne, Van Gogh, Le Corbusier, etc.

As happens with everything converted into mass consumption, he has been the object of much meddling and commercialization, of many factions and much patronizing, and thus has been reduced to a stereotyped idea, a myth, expressing all his interesting, complex and contradictory personality in a mere symbol.

In this sense the false idea of "Gaudí, the architect of the Sagrada Familia", or "The Sagrada Familia, the most important and only work of Gaudí", is offered, sold as a commercial product and accepted by more than a hundred million people throughout the world.

However, in spite of all this, when a person who is really interested in knowing about the work of the Catalan master, approaches his art humbly and with a modicum of sensitivity and intelligence, he will discover the true value of the powerful and pure gaudiesque world which has only been superficially scarred by publicity and the commercialization of his ideas.

The popularity and influence of great universal figures is normally based on real value, otherwise they would not resist the erosion that publicity, consumer commercialization and the passing of time inexorably subject them to.

Although popularity is not in itself a guarantee of intrinsic quality in a work of art, there is no doubt that when a work is good, all people are satisfied by its worth and general appeal. In the case of the Sagrada Familia three different aspects are superimposed upon each other, the religious, the political and the artistic; these, developed together with a considerable amount of feeling and integrity, have made the church a great popular success.

At different times, the three aspects mentioned have been valued in different ways. Thus, until 1900, Maragall defined it as "the cathedral of the poor" and the church committee kept their patronage of the work anonymous.

But with the coming to power of the middle class in the local and provincial authority in 1905, the Sagrada Familia became the New Cathedral of Greater Barcelona, incorporated into the Jaussely Plan and constituting and image of social reunification.

Finally, after being forgotten for a time during the Republic and after the fire and pillage it suffered in 1936, it has, after the civil war, become a new symbol that will reach its culmination in the 1982 Universal Exhibition when it is planned to finish the Façade of the Passion.

Detail of one of the tower balconies.

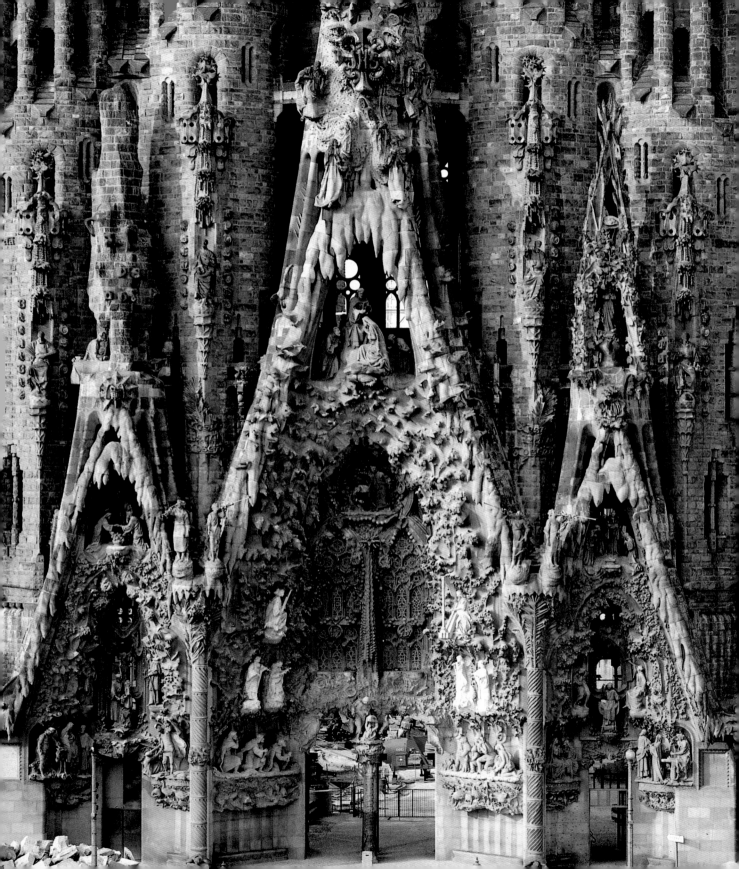

Baroque
exterior
contrasted
with the
geometry of
the interior
of the
Nativity
façade.

Due to the amount written on the Sagrada Familia, we think it necessary to give a summary of the commentaries on the photographs we have looked at. Emphasis has been placed on the sculpted groups from the Nativity façade due to their relative importance in the building.

At the same time, we have tried to contrast the two sides of this façade in order to clarify one part of the aforementioned summary.

The baroque character of the side facing the rising sun is an ideal framework for almost all the sculptures shown; while the geometrically simple and pure composition on the interior façade forms the counterpoint to the movement and chaos of its opponent.

The towers which were the last thing Gaudí did, are the theme treated in the last part of the summary on the Sagrada Familia.

The spiral structure of the towers and their staircases, which Gaudí liked so much that he considered that structure law in many sections of his architecture, together with the columns and steps etc. are part of a revolving parabola which defines its shape and which is statically perfect.

Cesar Martinell compared the towers of the Sagrada Familia to the human towers or "castells" that people make in the Penedés region, as their methods of maintaining balance are the same.

Finally, we show the great abstract sculptures radiant with venetian light, which are the tips of the towers.

As their composition is so complex Gaudí seems to have wanted to contrast them with the sculptures of a figurative-symbolic type on the lower part of the façade.

Fragments of the inner face of the Nativity façade.

Tips of the towers on the Sagrada Familia (pages 56-57). ▷

Interior view of one of the belltowers where tubular bells were to be hung.

Staircase leading down from the towers of the Nativity façade.

One stage in the building of the new façade of the
Sagrada Família.

Strangely enough, the structure of the towers on the Sagrada Familia is the same as that of the "human towers" of the "Xiquets de Valls".

*Detail of
the tips of
the towers.*

After the building of the Teresian College, in almost all Gaudí's works we find the typical tower with its three dimensional cross and four arms crowning the façade. With this cross a sort of subtle gaudiesque christianization was created rather in the style of the parish church or cathedral bells in the old city.

With the Sagrada Familia as a centre piece and the allegorical crosses of his buildings scattered over the city, they performed a symbolic role and projected Gaudí's religious ideology over all the surrounding city.

Religion, in Gaudí, is like his obsessive will to search and reach for perfection in his work.

His idea that the architect is a sort of high priest of his profession demonstrates how far his religious thought acted like a Wagnerian impulse to give his work that transcendental historical and philosophical quality.

Those of us who do not go along with the traditional interpretation of Gaudí cannot help thinking that his catholicism was no more than an historic method of satisfying his infinite desire for wisdom and his need to love and be loved.

From this point of view, the use of religion to make his art sacred constitutes an interesting case of ideological composition produced with some frequency in the history of art and culture as with Michaelangelo for example.

Nowadays, the traditional version offered by his good biographer Josep Rafols that it is only possible to understand Gaudí within the limits of religious faith, is a rather narrow interpretation considering the world wide popularity of his works and the fact that they have been understood and valued by people of widely different cultures and with other sets of values. This is why we must look for the basis for a complete understanding of the great Catalan master in his more universal and permanent qualities, and not in mere historical appreciations.

From the terraces of the Casa Milà and the Casa Batlló and from the Güell Park, the towers of the Sagrada Familia can be seen.

THE EPISCOPAL PALACE IN ASTORGA (1887-1894)

Commissioned by his friend and fellow countryman the Bishop of Astorga, Gaudí built this mansion using Catalan workmen brought specially to this old city on the route of St. James.

Gaudí was unable to finish the work due to the death of the Bishop. Therefore we cannot consider the upper floor and the roof as his work, for they were completely changed and did not allow for the construction of the magnificent roof which was conceived as a great pyramid strung with two rows of windows on its four sides.

The greyish white colour of the palace has lately been criticised for its contrast with the rose coloured hue of the neighbouring cathedral, but it has not been taken into account that with the pyramidical roof that would have dominated the building and the whiteness of the snow that would have covered it in winter, the harmony of colours would have been re-established.

◁ *Aerial view of the Bishop's Palace in Astorga.*

Interior of the Palace at present converted into the Way of Saint James Museum.

CASA DE LOS BOTINES. LEON
(1891-1894)

For a friend and client of Count Güell, the Fernandez-Arbós of León, textile merchants, Gaudí built a large mansion in the middle of the capital city, the ground floor and basement being designed as a warehouse for cloth, and the main part of the building as a residence for the owners, the remaining floors were let as flats.

It is surprising to see Gaudí working in León building a house in stone, a marked contrast to his former colourful phase in Barcelona.

The note of sobriety and simplicity of the façades on this house disappears in winter when, on snowy days, they look to be spotted with snow flakes adhering to the roughness of the stone which was left thus, so as to achieve this effect.

The Casa de los Botines, in León, viewed from St. Mark's square.

Entrance and detail of the façade.

Vantage point for viewing the Casa de Figueras or "Bellesguard" was once a shaded walk covered with parabolic arches linking the house with the garden.

Detail of the railing on the gate.

BELLESGUARD
(1900-1902)

In Catalan "Bellesguard" means "beautiful view" and it is certainly true that from this side of the Tibidabo lies one of the lovliest and most complete panoramic views to be seen in the magnificent combination of land and sea which makes up the city of Barcelona.

It was in this same place that King Martin I the humane had a house built for his pleasure.

Gaudí, in order to celebrate this fine view conceived the whole house as an immense pedestal with a fine observation room on top of the roof.

What was left of the royal residence was rebuilt, making an entrance to the estate and being included in the confines of the grounds, this was done by diverting the road leading to the Tibidabo mountain on this side.

To do this, he built a viaduct cum bulkhead to obviate a ravine running parallel to the road, supported by inclined columns which are a clumsy try-out for what he would later develop in a more masterful way in the Güell Park. The extraordinary thing about this small slender house is its perfect adaptation as regards colour to the green slopes of the mountain full of brush and pine trees which was achieved by building the house with the surrounding stone that had greyish green tones and together with the yellow moss made an effective colour scheme.

In contrast to the softness of the landscape, the aggressive line of wrought iron lances defending the entrance to the estate make a good definition of the concept of private property in the roman-catalan style.

The mythological aggressiveness of the dragon on the entrance to the Güell pavillions is here very apparent to whoever would like to disregard the sacred social implication of this in our region.

Axonometric projection of Bellesguard. (Source: E.T.S.A.B.)

GAUDI

The inside of the house is completely different from the gothic façades, which have been described as ghostly and dream-like. While in the case of the latter there may be some literary allusions yet to be explained, in the inside, Gaudí made an effort to affirm his own style and succeeded in doing so, as in the case of the Güell pavillions and the Teresian College. His personal style is mainly revealed in his treatment of the roofs, where, without abandoning his ideas on structure, he succeeds in creating spaces which are rational and emotive at the same time, due to his correct choice of materials, the knowledgeable composition of strong shapes and the adroit handling of indirect light and half light.

He tries out a different sort of roofing on each occasion by varying the brick arches and domes on the same theme. But the most excellent piece of work is to be found in the attic, which we have no doubt in qualifying as one of the most successful of all Gaudí's architectural creations.

There is so much to be said of the other parts of the house, for example, the magnificent courtyard at the entrance staircase, the sweep of the roof, the ingenious design of the wrought iron railings on the gate and on the windows of the ground floor, and so many other beautifully executed details...

Attic.

Entrance staircase.

Detail of a stained-glass
window.

Overall view of the courtyard
and inside staircase.

THE CASA CALVET
(1898-1904)

For yet another textile manufacturer, Pedro M. Calvet, Gaudí built this typical bourgeois house of the type in the Ensanche of Barcelona, very similar to that of Los Botines in León. In this house he begins the search for a fusion between the illuminating courtyards and the staircases, which he finally achieved in the Casa Batlló. The main façade, in our view, does not have the quality of the rear one where an original way of solving the problem of the galleries is developed.

Later façade of the Casa Calvet.   *Mirror in the entrance hall.*

Lift and
stairs
leading to
the floors.

Just as the treatment of the Bellesguard façade was an exercise in composition in the gothic style, in the Casa Calvet he is searching for the definition of his own personal style, trying out the possibilities offered him by baroque art which he had already tried out extensively on the Nativity façade and in the Rosary Chapel.

The large amount of furniture Gaudí designed for the Casa Calvet, that of the ground floor study in oak and that belonging to the owners' flat in upholstery shows what rapid progress he had made in the search for his own form of plastic art. Beginning with subjects of natural inspiration, he was to continue working on the difficult job of creating for the functional demands of modern furniture until he was able to produce the dining chairs for the Casa Batlló which are still admired for their complete modernity.

The greatest difficulties regarding precision in a characteristic style are to be found in those parts of a building which have a greater degree of freedom in composition as in the façades (let us recall the instance of the Güell pavilions and Bellesguard, where highly elaborate façades are contrasted with interiors which are structurally and in the plastic sense pure Gaudí).

It became possible to solve this problem when the difficulties relative to composition were dependent on the demands of the structure, the building or demands of a functional nature in clear and definite terms.

This is why, very early on, he was to achieve typically gaudiesque plastic structures, modern furniture or rational façades thanks to the pre-eminence of the method of balance or the aforementioned functional precision or when adornment was left in the background and only the functional considerations were of importance, as occurred with the rear façades of the Güell Palace and the Casa Calvet.

Chair from the study on the ground floor of the Casa Calvet. (Source: Gaudí Museum.)

Oak wood sofa from the study on the ground floor of the Casa Calvet. (Source: Gaudí Museum.)

Casa Batlló, on the right the Casa Amatller by Puig i Cadafalch.

Entrance hall on the ground floor.

Detail of the haunch of the stair banister.

Entrance staircase to the main floor.

Entrance staircase to the terrace.

Corridor in the attic.

Interior staircase courtyard.

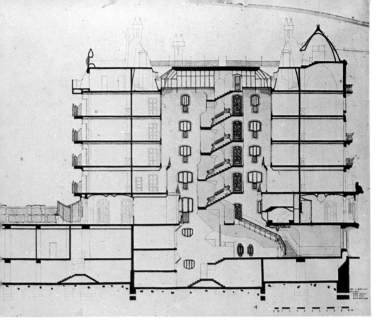

Longitudinal section. (Source: L. Bonet Garí).

For another bourgeois Catalan family, the textile manufacturers Batlló, Gaudí carried out the restoration of this old building situated in the Paseo de Gracia.

These are the years of his greatest public recognition. With the Sagrada Familia, the great collective enterprise of the Catalan bourgeoisie, and his civic works, Gaudí acquired much professional prestige and not a little envy; he is the undisputed master, imitated by architectural students in their degree theses.

Finally, once his highly personal style has become

Detail of the bay window on the ground floor.

consolidated through the years, he is able to apply it to almost every problem and all parts of a building, from the façades to the furnishings, bringing forth masterly ideas dictated exclusively by his own plastic art.

It is no longer necessary for him to resort to any historical styles, as this phase has been overcome, and he can devote himself to his marvellous interiors which are so new in the history of art and architecture. As an example, examine the photograph of the former dining room.

Inside view of the bay window. Background, Paseo de Gracia. Furniture belonging tot he former dining room and now in Gaudí Museum.

There is not sufficient space to give a minimal graphic or literary explanation of the importance of so many of the aspects of this building.

The superb staircase courtyard, whose light blends harmoniously through the blue tones of the glazed ceramic, covering the inner walls, has a series of windows, openings, and glass floors through which light penetrates from the lovely skylight down to the basement.

For the main floor, the best interior work of Gaudí's,

Chimney on the ground floor with masonry benches built in.

Main floor. Detail of lounge ceiling.

Matching armchairs from the old dining room, now in the Gaudí Museum.

he designed even the furniture, creating some of the most modern pieces from among the hundred or so different ones which he produced.

At the present time, only the front part of this floor has survived, as the magnificent dining room was destroyed and its furniture kept in the Gaudí House Museum in the Güell Park.

The fifteen most important works of Gaudí have been declared Historic and Artistic Monuments of National Interest.

Overall view of the terrace.

Detail of the dragon's backbone, with scales facing the Paseo de Gracia with tower and five armed crosses.

The attic and the terrace were constructed by Gaudí as a new floor of the old house, here he was able to apply his theory regarding the roofing of buildings. He held that buildings should have a double roof, just as important people have a hat and a sunshade. The roof should be built over an elastic structure different from the rest of the house, so that the changes brought about by the variations in temperature should be absorbed through this. Normally this elastic structure was made with diaphragmatic arches of brick as can be appreciated in the photographs on pages 71, 72, 81, and 110. His thorough apprenticeship in the handling of the ceramic surfacing demonstrated on the roofs of the entrance pavillions and on the staircase of the Güell Park —built between 1900 and 1903—, was taken advantage of in the Casa Batlló which gave Gaudí greater liberty as regards composition in the treatment of the chimneys sculpturally, in the dragon on the façade, in the treatment of the terminal cross and in the colour composition of the façade itself. At their due time, these works would serve to give him greater sureness and would spur him on to the creation of the bench in the Güell Park.

Rear view of the dragon's backbone.

Main staircase of the Güell Park. ▷

Main façade of the Güell Park with the porter's lodge in the foreground.

Left hand pavilion made for the administration of the unsuccessful private estate.

THE GÜELL PARK
(1900-1914)

The pavilion on the right was to be the porter's lodge and that on the left with a tower and a cross on top was to be an office building.

The high wall on the main façade closing the precinct served rather a psychological purpose: that of giving the inhabitants security and protection because at the beginning of the century, this area was somewhat isolated.

Count Güell in order to reinforce this feeling had a headquarters for the Civil Guard built right at side of the Park and donated it to them.

Axonometric projection of Güell Park made by Ramon Bosch. (Source: A.H.U.A.D.)

If Gaudí's exceptional gifts were to be seen in so many works, it was thanks to the help and support always given him by Don Eusebio Güell i Bacigalupi, a refined and generous nobleman who played his part of patron at the same level of genius as his illustrious protegé.

Mutual friendship, respect and admiration guaranteed a fruitful collaboration between the two.

Gaudí's relations with the Güells, the most wealthy family in the whole Catalonia did, on the other hand, put him in contact with the cream of society and thanks to the relationships existing between these people he was able, even for reasons of a snobbish nature, to receive their favours and commissions.

Count Güell admired the English garden cities of which he had direct knowledge, so he decided to instigate the creation of a garden suburb of an exclusively residential nature. For this, he commissioned Gaudí for the work on the substructure and fundamental organization so as to attract the attention of future residents.

When he created the Güell Park, Gaudí made the only really new model of urban art in the modernist epoch.

For this, he opened up the pedestrian traffic on the walks, making different lanes and a pedestrian path in the shape of a staircase, along with lanes with varying degrees of slope compared with the main road, which was for carriages and cars, having a maximum of 6° slope.

At times the pedestrian and the vehicular routes co-incided, so while the viaducts were for the traffic passing above, below, under the columns were covered porches where one was protected from the sun, or rain for part of the way leading to the different plots.

So the plan was devised to build only in sunny areas, which allowed enormous green spaces of incomprehensible proportions for our present day mentality: more than 50 % of the total surface area of the park.

The plots were triangular in shape and distributed quincunx so that the houses built in the middle of the triangle should not obstruct the views over Barcelona for those built behind.

As regards facilities, he built a large square whose lower part was to be for a market and the upper part a Theatre of Nature, recreation centre and a centre for any cultural or social happenings anyone wished to celebrate.

At the same time, the large square served as a surface for the collection of rain water, that is why a large cistern was placed under the porticoes of the market with a capacity of more than 12,000 m^2 for the use of the community.

Sculptural detail of a central element in the main stair.

Underview of the columns, taken from the main staircase of the Güell Park with the covered bench in the foreground.

Axonometric projection of the square and the lower colonnade with the earth covering it taken away. On the right, are the drains for the square inside the columns which can be used for filling the cistern. (Source: Salvador Tarragó and Ramón Bosch.)

Colonnade.

Decorative soffit of an architrave — work of J. Jujol — suspended below the square.

In spite of so much foresight and the extraordinary quality of the new environment offered to the new residents, the experiment failed financially; only two plots were sold, one of these being bought by Gaudí himself.

The Güell Park remained as a private garden until the twenties when the descendents of Don Eusebio Güell handed it over to the Municipality to be used as a public garden.

Fragments of the bench in the Güell Park.

Interior views of the Güell Park viaducts destined for pedestrians.

The Güell Park was built in two stages, during the first (1900-1903) everything except the long undulating bench in the square was built; the aforementioned bench was made between 1907 and 1912 approximately.

It is surprising to think that the movement in this bench was obtained by prefabricated pieces formed into plastered domes and covered with tiles, a procedure which was also used for building some parts of the entrance pavillions, stairs and lower colonnade.

But Gaudí the foresighted city architect and innovator (he used concrete for building the Park for the first time ever in Spain), did not limit his creative work to these technical aspects, but, along with them, conceived spaces of such extraordinary quality that on the shores of the Mediterranean, few architectural-urban units look towards to sea with such solidarity, strength and dignity as this in the Güell Park.

In the composition of the domes on the colonnade and in the covering of certain parts of the bench, Gaudí had the collaboration of the most gifted of his students in the sphere of plastic art, the outstanding architect, José M.ª Jujol, with whom he created, by means of bits of ceramic, glass and bottles, some extraordinary "collages" which were ten years in advance of abstract and surrealist painting. It is inconceivable how, being far away from any contact with the experiments of the European vanguardists, both architects revealed a new world of shapes of such quality that 60 years later, they have not been improved upon.

In order to get the appropriate section for the bench Gaudí made a naked workman sit on a layer of plaster and once he had this profile he was able to finish off the bench. The closed or open incurvations shown occur according to how they follow the capitals of the lower columns —which the bench finishes off— either diagonally or parallel to the square on which they are placed.

Underground walk-viaduct. The vaults are of brick covered with stone.

THE SAGRADA FAMILIA SCHOOL (1909-1910)

Interior view of the school. (Photo: Mas Archive.)

In the year 1909, as a foretaste of what future parish schools built under the protection of the church once it was finished, should be, these schools were built in the same place as where the main façade of the Sagrada Familia had to be. Was this an unconfessed desire on the part of the architect to avoid finishing the Temple? By using simple brick partition-walls conveniently curved —so as to get maximum resistence and stability, with a minimum of material— and having a roof, also made of various thicknesses of brick and masterfully undulated, a small work of art was created.

This simple construction made such an impression on Le Corbusier in 1928, that when, in 1951, he tried to resolve the roofing for the Law Courts in Chandigar, this small roof inspired him with the correct solution to his problem.

Aerial view of the roof. It is just possible to see the counterposed movement of the façade. To appreciate this, observe the upper part of the old photograph.

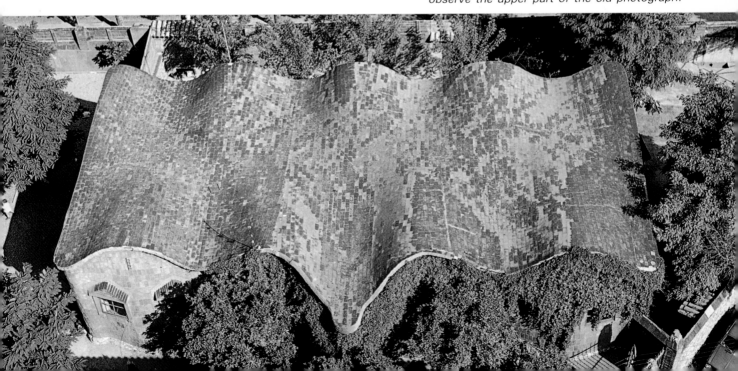

Aerial view of the Casa Milà where it's quite possible to see its architectural and urban organization; the two large inner courtyards, the movement of the façade and the courtyard inside the building, etc.

THE CASA MILA (1906-1910)

With ''La Pedrera'', the name by which this building is popularly known, Gaudí, thanks to his masterly solutions to problems, to the inventions he makes, and to the quality of his finishes, shows himself to be an inexhaustable genius, with an enormous creative capacity which makes each work of his totally different from the preceding one, and, if possible, better in quality.

Details on the façade.

Great artists have always possessed their own active interpretation of Nature precisely because their work consists in transforming it.

Gaudí's statement that..."originality is going back to the origin" is merely a way of expressing his thought on a subject which implies getting to know and discovering the laws of nature in order to make use of them and to continue the work of the Creator which means to create a second human nature. La Pedrera is the plastic and architectural demonstration of his concept of Nature. Collins defines it as "a mountain built by the hand of Man". Indeed, this colossal architectural cliff with holes, with its enormous movement on the façade like a rough and immovable sea of stone together with "the tempering colour of the stone, adorned with climbing plants and flowers on the balconies which would have brought constant touches of varied colour to the house", as Gaudí himself said, it constitutes the strongest expression of the romantic, anticlassical will to naturalize architecture.

This will is the same as the reverse effort to architecturalize Nature represented by the Güell Park. With this building, the best, in our view, of all Barce-

Fragment of the railings in the courtyard overlooking the Paseo de Gracia.

Entrance. ▷

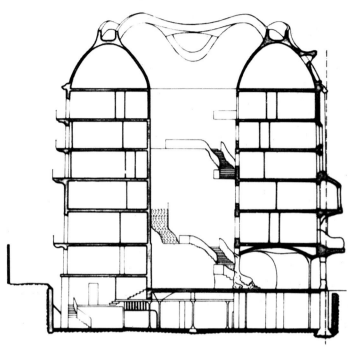

Inside view of the courtyard on the Calle Provenza.
(Photo: Patricio Vélez.)

Roof of the main floor. (Photo: Patricio Vélez.)

Section of the Casa Milà according to plans. Observe
the staircase as it winds around the courtyard, and
how the house is supported by columns.

Interior views of the attic
before being altered.
(Photo: Mas Archive.)

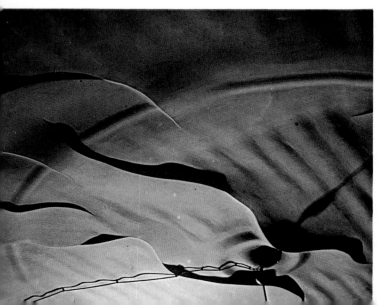

lona's civic architecture, there closes an important stage in the History of architecture: the stage which, beginning at the Renaissance, ends with the nineteenth century.

The historical mission of liquidating the classical inheritance is genially accomplished by this giant of the art of construction, by closing one door on the history of culture he opens another: that which leads to the twentieth century, which will have as its architectural symbol the monument of Tatlin and will be defined in the "Unité d'habitation" of Le Corbusier in Marseille.

Gaudí, in the Casa Milá, appears to be trying to finish with the traditional concept of a block of flats and give birth to a new type of residence. But he is only partly successful, as this was to be the study and the work of another generation with more advanced social and urban problems and with a different scale of values and a more highly evolved social reality.

If he had had more land to build on, Gaudí, doubtless, would have constructed a double spiral ramp round an enormous courtyard allowing cars to reach the roof terrace.

How would this house have looked if it had been possible to build car parks inside it with a surface area of more than 400 square metres for each flat distributed on two or three floors? How could he superimpose palace-residences around an enormous courtyard?

However, as it was impossible to have a piece of land of 2.000 square metres, he put in its place a spiral staircase which, winding round the inside walls of the courtyard, would reach the living parts (in practice he only built an external staircase up to the second floor) and also a ramp reaching the basement for parking cars and carriages.

The whole house is held up by stone or brick columns and metal trellis-work, there being no reinforcing walls. As the partition walls in the rooms are very simple to put up and take down the building is able to adapt to any new use, as an hotel for example.

Looking at the inner courtyards, the regular distribution of the pillars is perfectly clearly seen on the inside façades, but this regularity does not exist inside as the pillars are distributed extremely freely, up to the point that at times they are not prolonged vertically as in the lower parts of the courtyard in the Calle Provenza.

The degree of complexity of a structure of this nature is such that only one with the intelligence of a Gaudí could conceive of building it.

Another fundamental aspect of La Pedrera is the fact that Gaudí succeeded in destroying the architecture of the façade by using an antifaçade building, a building without any traditional rule of composition and only governed by the subliminal law which gives rise to this magnanimous naturalism, leaving the way free for the conception of the building without façade (the curtain wall which Le Corbusier was to formulate as one of the five points of the programme defining modern architecture).

It is because of all we have mentioned that the Casa Milá reveals this contradictory character presenting problems in advance of its age, as are the "pilotis", the roof show, the almost non existent façade, the free floor, the surrealistic plastic art etc., at the same time some other things are out of tune.

Bourgeois residences of 400 square metres are not suitable programmes for experiments in new ways of life in a modern city.

Whether or not he was conscious of all the contradictory and problematic nature of the question which progressively departed from the initial project and became more and more conventional, Gaudí abandoned the work unfinished and adulterated in the hands of less capable colleagues such as Pujol and Sugrañes. For his last sixteen years Gaudí shut himself up in the Sagrada Familia seeking the answer in religious architecture to a perhaps nineteenth century concept of architecture.

The roof terrace of La Pedrera constitutes the best abstract-surrealist scenario ever created in the history of architecture.

It is like the final eclosion of this tumultuous subterranean world of Gaudí's subconscious which has been so little studied.

With the steps placed close to the edge of deep courtyards, and the dizziness created by the absence of banisters and the consequent insecurity and psychological defencelessness produced on the visitors, it created the right state of mind for the monsters and enigmatic hooded people to have their maximum effect.

The terrace on completion and as it is now.
(Source: Puig Boada.)

View of the chimneys and exits onto the terrace. ▷

Ventilators on the Casa Milà.

THE GÜELL COLONY
(1898-1915)

In Santa Coloma de Cervelló, Count Güell built a textile factory and a workers' colony beside it. Apparently, Francisco Berenguer, one of Gaudí's collaborators took charge of the development of the colony and some of the buildings, while Guadí devoted himself to the construction of the best of his works, the church belonging to the colony.

It is situated at the foot ot a little hill in the middle of a wood and Gaudí calculated both the journey to the church and its architectural integration into the landscape. To build this church, initiated in 1908 and interrupted in 1915, Gaudí used a system of construction of long standing in Catalonia which were domes made from brick and plaster. But the use of these materials did not imply a traditional treatment of these elastic structures, rather an incredible development of their possibilities which brought out new inventions and applications as those of the hyperbolic parabolas. Therefore, the crypt constitutes a complete inventory of all the structures it is possible to obtain with the use of the brick.

Terrace steps for reaching the main part of the church. To the left, the entrance to the crypt.

Fragment of the illumination windows in the crypt. ▷

View of the whole and detail of the interior of the Güell colony church. Observe how it is coloured over the respective photos of the model so as to get an overall view.

From 1898 till 1908, Gaudí was studying the project for the church using a model made from string which materialized the axes of the columns and the archways, and from which hung little bags of lead shot whose weight was in proportion to the stress they had to bear.

With this proceedure, he acquired the inverted mechanical structure which, once photographed was then painted to see the resulting spatial effect. If the inside photographs are examined closely, it is possible to see, under the gouache that has been removed, the threads of the model.

With this direct method, which he was to use later to completely remake the structure of the naves in the Sagrada Familia, Gaudí culminated a long search of almost thirty years for the most appropriate resistant forms for the resolution of structures working under compression, as normally are stone constructions.

His firm will to overcome the Gothic, which had obsessed him from a young man, had now been

Entrance porch to the crypt. The brick vaults are noteworthy; they are parabolic hyperbolic in shape and appear to be suspended.

achieved fully, both in structure and in form.

Gaudí's lack of interest in the urban theme of the colony contrasts with his youthful attitude of pre-occupation for these subjects.

On the other hand, he, who had worked on this church for twenty years and had spent forty two dedicated to the Sagrada Familia, showed that the architectural resolution of the theme of the Temple was of prime importante for him, as it was to be for the history of architecture. But, with the social changes of the twentieth century, the church, as a theme, has decreased in importance, and, for

example, parliament has acquired increasing importance.

His definite abandonment of architecture around 1910 and his absolute dedication to the Sagrada Familia and to this small church, show his renunciation of study and his solving of crucial problems which modern civilization posed in architecture, and also his dramatic cloistering up in a sort of cul de sac. With this, we do not pre-judge the artistic value of his magnificent results, but merely limit ourselves to valuing the social and historical significance of Gaudí's attitude.

Inside of the crypt.

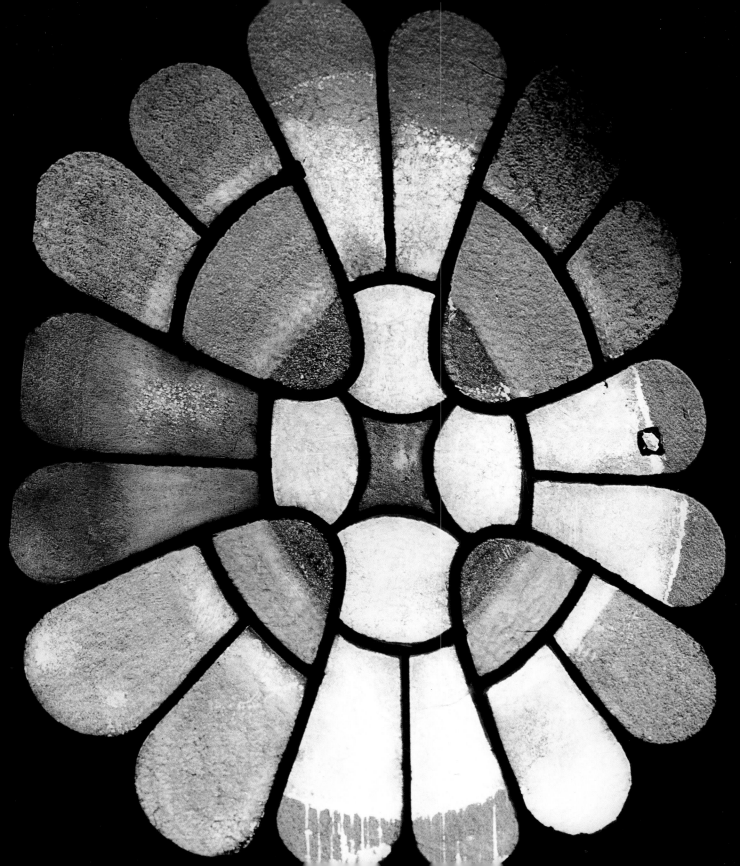

(Source: Urban Commission.)

THE SITUATION OF GAUDI'S WORKS IN BARCELONA AND DISTRICT.

1 THE CIUDADELA PARK
2 THE STREET LAMPS IN THE PLAZA REAL
3 THE CASA VICENS
4 THE GÜELL PAVILIONS
5 THE TERESIAN COLLEGE
6 THE GÜELL PALACE
7 THE SAGRADA FAMILIA

8 BELLESGUARD
9 THE CASA CALVET
10 THE CASA BATLLO
11 THE GÜELL PARK
12 THE CASA MILA
13 THE GÜELL COLONY

Considered as a whole, the work of this Jupiter Ammon of architecture can be divided into four clearly different stages. 1878-1882. From when he finished his career as an architect at the Barcelona School of Architects, until he began to build the Casa Vicens, is the stage we have named civic works.

1883-1900 approximately. The decorative stage in which he seeks to overcome eclecticism and embarks upon the following buildings: Casa Vicens, Güell pavilions, El Capricho, the Güell Palace, the Sagrada Familia, the Episcopal Palace in Astorga, Casa de los Botines, Bellesguard and Casa Calvet. 1900-1917. He creates his own style and contributes the following to history, the Güell Park, Casa Batlló, Casa Milá, the schools of the Sagrada Familia and the church in the Güell Colony. 1918-1926. The stage of complete dedication to the Sagrada Familia, characterized by a supreme geometric preoccupation whose most important products are the tips of the Nativity façade towers. We summarize the extensive bibliography to allow those interested to widen their knowledge of Gaudí: *Nueva visión de Gaudí* by E. Casanelles. Barcelona: La Polígrafa. 1965, is the best human analysis of Gaudí, followed by *Gaudí* by J. Ráfols. Barcelona: Ed. Canosa. 1929.

Also of interest is *Gaudí, assaig biogràfic* by J. Elias. Barcelona: Ed. Circo. 1961. From a technical point of view, the most comprehensive are: *Gaudí, su vida su teoría, su obra.* Barcelona. College of Architects of Catalonia and the Balaerics. 1967: *Antoni Gaudí, l'home i l'obra* by J. Bergós. Barcelona: Ariel. 1954 and *Antoni Gaudí* by R. Pane. Milan: Ed. di Comunità. 1964. As a fine summary: *Antonio Gaudí* by G. R. Collins. Barcelona. Ed. Bruguera. 1961 and also of interest are *Gaudí* by J. Bassegoda Nonell. Madrid: Publicaciones españolas. 1971. *El temple de la Sagrada Familia* by I. Puig Boada. Barcelona. 1929 and 1952. Also *La visión artística y religiosa de Gaudí* by R. Descharnes and others. Barcelona: Aymá. 1969.

Fundamental for any study or reference is the complete Gaudí bibliography and the Catalan modernism: *Antonio Gaudí and the Catalan Movement. 1870-1930* by G. R. Collins. Charlottesville: Ed. W. B. O'Neal. TAAAB. 1973.

Contents

Collection ALL EUROPE

	Spanish	French	English	German	Italian	Catalan	Dutch	Swedish	Portuguese	Japanese	Finnish
1 ANDORRA	●	●	●	●	●	●					
2 LISBON	●	●	●	●	●				●		
3 LONDON	●	●	●	●	●						●
4 BRUGES	●	●	●	●	●		●				
5 PARIS	●	●	●	●	●					●	
6 MONACO	●	●	●	●	●					●	
7 VIENNA	●	●	●	●	●			●		●	
8 NICE	●	●	●	●	●						
9 CANNES	●	●	●	●							
10 ROUSSILLON	●	●	●	●		●					
11 VERDUN	●	●	●	●							
12 THE TOWER OF LONDON	●	●	●	●	●		●				
13 ANTWERP	●	●	●	●	●						
14 WESTMINSTER ABBEY	●	●	●	●	●						
15 THE SPANISH RIDING SCHOOL IN VIENNA	●	●	●	●	●						
16 FATIMA	●	●	●	●					●		
17 WINDSOR CASTLE	●	●	●	●	●					●	
18 THE OPAL COAST		●	●								
19 COTE D'AZUR	●	●	●	●	●						
20 AUSTRIA	●	●	●	●	●						

Currently being prepared

	Spanish	French	English	German	Italian	Catalan	Dutch	Swedish	Portuguese	Japanese	Finnish
21 LOURDES	●	●	●	●	●	●					
22 BRUSSELS	●	●	●	●	●						
23 SCHÖNBRUNN PALACE	●	●	●	●	●				●		
24 ROUTE OF PORT WINE	●	●	●	●							
25 CYPRUS			●	●		●					
26 HOFBURG PALACE	●	●	●	●	●						
27 ALSACE	●	●	●	●	●		●				

Currently being prepared

	Spanish	French	English	German	Italian	Catalan	Dutch	Swedish	Portuguese	Japanese	Finnish
28 RHODES											
29 BERLIN											
30 CORFU			●	●	●						
31 MALTA		●									
32 PERPIGNAN											

Currently being prepared

	Spanish	French	English	German	Italian	Catalan	Dutch	Swedish	Portuguese	Japanese	Finnish
33 STRASBOURG											
34 MADEIRA											
35 CERDAGNE - CAPCIR		●			●						
36 CARCASSONE											
37 AVIGNON											

Currently being prepared

Collection ART IN SPAIN

Now being revised

	Spanish	French	English	German	Italian	Catalan	Dutch	Swedish	Portuguese	Japanese	Finnish
1 PALAU DE LA MUSICA CATALANA (Catalan Palace of Music)	●	●	●	●	●					●	
2 GAUDI	●	●	●	●	●					●	
3 PRADO MUSEUM I (Spanish Painting)	●	●	●	●	●						
4 PRADO MUSEUM II (Foreign Painting)	●	●	●	●	●						
5 MONASTERY OF GUADALUPE	●										
6 THE CASTLE OF XAVIER	●	●	●	●	●					●	
7 THE FINE ARTS MUSEUM OF SEVILLE	●	●	●	●	●						
8 SPANISH CASTLES	●	●	●	●							
9 THE CATHEDRALS OF SPAIN	●	●	●	●							
10 THE CATHEDRAL OF GERONA	●	●	●	●							

Now being revised
Currently being prepared

	Spanish	French	English	German	Italian	Catalan	Dutch	Swedish	Portuguese	Japanese	Finnish
11 GRAN TEATRE DEL LICEU DE BARCELONA (The Great Opera House)											
12 THE ROMANESQUE STYLE IN CATALONIA	●	●	●	●							
13 LA RIOJA: ART TREASURES AND WINE-GROWING RESOURCES	●	●	●	●						●	
14 PICASSO	●	●	●	●	●						
15 REALES ALCAZARES (ROYAL PALACE OF SEVILLE)	●	●	●	●	●						
16 MADRID'S ROYAL PALACE	●	●	●	●	●						
17 ROYAL MONASTERY OF EL ESCORIAL	●	●	●	●	●						
18 THE WINES OF CATALONIA	●										
19 THE ALHAMBRA AND THE GENERALIFE	●	●	●	●	●						
20 GRANADA AND THE ALHAMBRA (ARAB AND MAURESQUE MONUMENTS OF CORDOVA, SEVILLE AND GRANADA)											
21 ROYAL ESTATE OF ARANJUEZ											
22 ROYAL ESTATE OF EL PARDO											
23 ROYAL HOUSES	●	●	●	●	●						
24 ROYAL PALACE OF SAN ILDEFONSO	●	●	●	●	●						
25 HOLY CROSS OF THE VALLE DE LOS CAIDOS	●	●	●	●	●						
26 OUR LADY OF THE PILLAR OF SARAGOSSA											
27 MORELLA											

Currently being prepared

Collection ALL SPAIN

	Spanish	French	English	German	Italian	Catalan	Dutch	Swedish	Portuguese	Japanese	Finnish
1 ALL MADRID	●	●	●	●	●					●	
2 ALL BARCELONA	●	●	●	●	●						
3 ALL SEVILLE	●	●	●	●	●					●	
4 ALL MAJORCA	●	●	●	●	●						
5 ALL THE COSTA BRAVA	●	●	●	●	●						
6 ALL MALAGA and the Costa del Sol	●	●	●	●	●		●				
7 ALL THE CANARY ISLANDS, Gran Canaria, Lanzarote and Fuerteventura	●	●	●	●	●		●	●			
8 ALL CORDOBA	●	●	●	●	●					●	
9 ALL GRANADA	●	●	●	●	●		●				
10 ALL VALENCIA	●	●	●	●	●					●	
11 ALL TOLEDO	●	●	●	●	●					●	
12 ALL SANTIAGO	●	●	●	●	●						
13 ALL IBIZA and Formentera	●	●	●	●	●						
14 ALL CADIZ and the Costa de la Luz	●	●	●	●	●						
15 ALL MONTSERRAT	●	●	●	●	●						
16 ALL SANTANDER and Cantabria	●		●								
17 ALL THE CANARY ISLANDS II, Tenerife, La Palma, Gomera, Hierro	●	●	●	●	●						

Currently being prepared

	Spanish	French	English	German	Italian	Catalan	Dutch	Swedish	Portuguese	Japanese	Finnish
18 ALL ZAMORA											
19 ALL PALENCIA											
20 ALL BURGOS, Covarrubias and Santo Domingo de Silos	●	●	●	●	●						
21 ALL ALICANTE and the Costa Blanca	●	●	●	●	●		●				
22 ALL NAVARRA	●	●	●	●							
23 ALL LERIDA, Province and Pyrenees	●	●	●	●		●					
24 ALL SEGOVIA and Province	●	●	●	●	●						
25 ALL SARAGOSSA and Province	●	●	●	●	●					●	
26 ALL SALAMANCA and Province	●	●	●	●	●						
27 ALL AVILA and Province	●	●	●	●							
28 ALL MINORCA	●	●	●	●	●						
29 ALL SAN SEBASTIAN and Guipúzcoa	●										
30 ALL ASTURIAS	●										
31 ALL LA CORUNNA and the Rías Altas	●	●	●	●							
32 ALL TARRAGONA and Province	●	●	●	●							
33 ALL MURCIA and Province	●	●	●	●							
34 ALL VALLADOLID and Province	●	●									
35 ALL GIRONA and Province	●	●									
36 ALL HUESCA and Province	●	●	●	●							
37 ALL JAEN and Province	●	●	●	●							
38 ALL ALMERIA and Province	●	●	●	●							

Currently being prepared

	Spanish	French	English	German	Italian	Catalan	Dutch	Swedish	Portuguese	Japanese	Finnish
39 ALL CASTELLON and the Costa del Azahar											
40 ALL CUENCA and Province	●	●	●	●							
41 ALL LEON and Province	●	●	●	●							
42 ALL PONTEVEDRA, VIGO and the Rías Bajas	●	●	●	●							
43 ALL RONDA	●	●	●	●	●						
44 ALL SORIA											

Currently being prepared

	Spanish	French	English	German	Italian	Catalan	Dutch	Swedish	Portuguese	Japanese	Finnish
45 ALL HUELVA	●										
46 ALL EXTREMADURA	●	●	●	●							
47 ALL ANDALUSIA	●	●	●	●							

Currently being prepared
48 ALL GALICIA ____ Currently being prepared
49 ALL CATALONIA ____ Currently being prepared
50 ALL LA RIOJA ____ Currently being prepared
51 ALL LUGO ____

Collection ALL AMERICA

	Spanish	French	English	German	Italian	Catalan	Dutch	Swedish	Portuguese	Japanese	Finnish
1 PUERTO RICO	●		●								
2 SANTO DOMINGO	●		●								
3 QUEBEC			●	●							
4 COSTA RICA	●		●								

Collection ALL AFRICA

	Spanish	French	English	German	Italian	Catalan	Dutch	Swedish	Portuguese	Japanese	Finnish
1 MOROCCO	●	●	●	●	●						
2 THE SOUTH OF MOROCCO	●	●	●	●	●						
3 TUNISIA		●	●	●	●						

Text, photographs, lay-out, design and printing by EDITORIAL ESCUDO DE ORO, S.A.
Rights of total or partial reproduction and translation reserved.
Copyright of this edition for photographs and text: © EDITORIAL ESCUDO DE ORO, S.A.
14th Edition, March 1992 - I.S.B.N. 84-378-0146-X - Dep. Legal B. 9933-1992

Printed in EEC by FISA - Escudo de Oro, S.A.